Red Cycle

Bible

Skills Drills & Thrills

A Fun Filled Bible Skills Curriculum

Writers

Joanna Moore Donna Arnold Rhonda VanCleave Deanna White GG Mathis Gail Scheffers
LifeWay Press® Nashville, Tennessee

ISBN: 9781430035978
Item 005690671

Dewy Decimal Classification Number: 220
Subject Heading: BIBLE-USE

Printed in the United States of America

Kids Ministry Publishing
LifeWay Church Resources
One LifeWay Plaza
Nashville, Tennessee 37234-0172

We believe that the Bible has God for its author; salvation for its end; and truth, without any mixture of error, for its matter and that all Scripture is totally true and trustworthy. To review LifeWay's doctrinal guideline, please visit *www.lifeway.com/doctrinalguideline*.

Table of Contents

Dear Parents,

We are happy to have your child be a part of Bible Skills, Drills, & Thrills.

Few things are more life changing than for a child to have knowledge of God's Word and the ability to use the Bible effectively. In addition, your child will have an opportunity to learn the books of the Bible, Bible book content, Bible history, Bible people, and life application.

Each week children will spend time learning Bible verses, the books of the Bible, and Key Passage titles and references. This year children will learn 25 verses and 10 Key Passages. You will find a poster showing the books of the Bible on page 77 and a Skills Check List on page 79. You can encourage your child by posting these in a prominent place.

We will use a variety of fun games and activities to teach the Bible skills and Bible material. Activities may include an active game, a quiet game, puzzles, a simple craft, or a writing activity. The group time will include a Bible story, prayer, verse memorization, practice using their Bibles, and life application of the story and verses. Children may choose between four hands-on application options: Bible Skills, Recreation, Crafts, or Service. All choices relate to the Bible material.

Each of the 36 meetings will conclude with a special Family Bible Skills to Go time. We hope that you will be able to attend this 5-10 minutes to learn more about what your child is learning.

We look forward to having your child be a part of our group.

In Christ's Name,

Psalm 119:105

The Bible from A to Z

Work with your group to describe the Bible using words that begin with each letter of the alphabet. The two most difficult ones are done for you.

A
B
C
D
E
F
G
H
I
J
K
L

M
N
O
P
Q
R
S
T
U
V
W

Xposes sin

Y

Zooms in on God's love.

Bible Firsts

Can you name some of the "firsts" that are mentioned in the book of Genesis? You may use your Bible to find the answers.

1. What was created by God in the beginning? (Genesis 1:1) _____

2. Who was the first gardener? (Genesis 2:15) _____

3. Who did the first surgery? (Genesis 2:21) _____

4. What was the first sin? (Genesis 3:6) _____

5. Who was the first mother? (Genesis 4:1) _____

6. Who was the first baby? (Genesis 4:1) _____

7. Who was the first shepherd? (Genesis 4:2) _____

8. Who was the first murderer? (Genesis 4:8) _____

9. Who was the first child named before birth? (Genesis 16:11) _____

10. Who was the first mother to have twins? (Genesis 25:21-24) _____

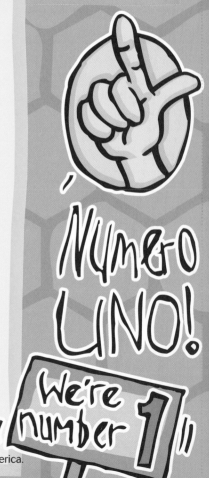

NUMERO UNO!

We're number 1

Self Portrait

Meeting 2

Draw a head and shoulders picture of yourself in the picture frame.
Using the words from Genesis 1:27, fill in the blanks in the thought balloon.

Write the 10 words you can think of that best describe you.

1.

2.

3.

4.

5.

6.

7.

8.

9.

10.

I AM IMPORTANT

BECAUSE GOD _____

ME IN _____ _____.

Creation Word Search

God not only created plants, animals, people, sky, and seas, He also created the processes necessary to sustain life on earth. In the word search, find nine things God created. Discuss with your leader how these things work together for the good of all creation.

A	M	K	W	P	L	A	N	T	S
M	W	A	T	E	R	B	D	M	L
L	R	N	S	O	I	L	R	P	I
C	E	I	G	P	K	S	M	T	G
A	H	M	W	L	T	N	V	R	H
R	G	A	F	E	R	U	L	E	T
B	O	L	P	O	X	Y	G	E	N
O	K	S	M	H	W	R	K	S	E
N	D	I	O	X	I	D	E	F	K

Fingerprint Critters

Your fingerprints are unique. That means that no one has the same fingerprints as you. Even identical twins have different fingerprints.

Use a stamp pad and a sheet of paper to create some of these fingerprint critters.

Bible Skills, Drills, & Thrills Activity Book Grades 4–6 Red Cycle
© 2014 LifeWay Press®--Printed in the United States of America.

Crack the Code

Two Key Passages and their references are written in code. Can you crack the code and match the reference with its Key Passage:

SGD BQDZSHNM

SGD FQDZS
BNLLZMCLDMSR

FDMDRHR 0-1:2

LZQJ 11:27-33

Letter Code

A = B	E = F	I = J	M = N	Q = R	U = V	Y = Z
B = C	F = G	J = K	N = O	R = S	V = W	Z = A
C = D	G = H	K = L	O = P	S = T	W = X	
D = E	H = I	L = M	P = Q	T = U	X = Y	

Number Code

Add 1 to each number.
Example:
John 2:15 = John 3:16

Test Your Commandment IQ!

1. Which of the following groups wanted to get rid of Jesus?
A. Pharisees   C. Herodians   E. All of them
B. Sadducees   D. Scribes

2. What question did one of the scribes ask to try to trick Jesus?
A. Who gave you the authority to teach?
B. Should we pay taxes to Rome?
C. Which commandment is the most important of all?

3. How did Jesus answer the scribe's question?
A. All the commandments are equally important.
B. The Ten Commandments are the most important.
C. First, love God. Then love your neighbor as much as you love yourself.

4. What was the scribe's reaction to Jesus' reply?
A. You are right, Teacher!
B. I disagree with you.
C. What about God's other commands?

5. What does it mean to love God with your heart, soul, mind, and strength?
_____

6. What does it mean to love your neighbor as yourself? _____
_____

Bible Skills, Drills, & Thrills Activity Book Grades 4–6 Red Cycle © 2014 LifeWay Press®--Printed in the United States of America.

Meeting 4
The Israelites Leave Egypt

Across

3. The Israelites had been in Egypt _____ hundred thirty years. (verse 41)
4. The Israelites took _____ made of gold and silver from the Egyptians. (verse 35)
7. Cattle, _____, and herds left with the Israelites. (verse 38)
9. What time of day did Pharaoh call for Moses and Aaron? _____ (verse 31)

Down

1. The Israelites left from _____. (verse 37)
2. Pharaoh asked Moses to _____ him as the people left Egypt. (verse 32)
3. The Lord struck all the _____ in Egypt. (verse 29)
5. About six hundred _____ men left Egypt. (verse 37)
6. The people would remember this night because it was the night God brought them out of the land of _____. (verse 42)
8. The people took unleavened cakes of _____ with them. (verse 39)

This is a Test

Your name: _____

Read the entire page before writing anything. You will learn that instructions are meant to be followed. Often things are difficult because people do not follow instructions. It takes time to read, understand, and follow instructions. But skipping the instructions is not wise. When you finish, sit quietly until time is called.

1. Write your name in the space provided above.

2. Draw a circle around your name.

3. Draw five small squares in the upper right corner of this page.

4. Put an "X" in each square.

5. Underline This Is a Test.

6. After This Is a Test write OK.

7. Draw a circle around each word in direction number 6.

8. Say your first name aloud before writing any more on this test.

9. If you think you have followed all directions up to this point, call out, "I have."

10. Put your first name in the middle of the bottom of this page.

11. Now that you have read everything before writing anything as you were instructed in the first paragraph, do only sentences 1 and 10.

Meeting 5

Scrambled Books

Unscramble each of these Old Testament Books of Law and History. When you have finished, write a number beside each book to indicate the order it appears in the Old Testament. Use your Bible to check your work.

DUGSEJ

2 MULESA

1 HICLESCRON

ROOMYTEENUD

SINGEES

1 SINGK

THERES

THRU

LIVESUITC

SHUJOA

AIMHEHEN

2 HICLESCRON

SOXEDU

2 SINGK

RAZE

BUMERSN

1 MULESA

File   Edit   View   Insert   Format   Font   Tools   Table   Window   Work   Help

Psalm 105:1-15

1. Compare these verses with 1 Chronicles 16:8-22.
2. Find at least three ways this Psalm gives to praise God for keeping His promises.

I can know that God will remember His promises to me even if I forget mine to Him.

God is worthy of praise and worship.

Psalm 96

1. Compare this Psalm with 1 Chronicles 16:23-33.
2. Find at least three ways to praise God in this Psalm.

Psalm 106

1. Find the three verses from Psalm 106 that appear in 1 Chronicles 16:34-36.
2. Find at least three ways in this Psalm that the people disobeyed God.

Bible Skills, Drills, & Thrills Activity Book Grades 4–6 Red Cycle © 2014 LifeWay Press®--Printed in the United States of America.

The Number's Up

39	2	27
12	5	66

Choose a number from the box to correctly complete each statement:

1. Number of books in the Poetry division_____.
2. Number of books in the Old Testament _____.
3. Number of books in Old Testament History division

    _____.

4. Number of books in the New Testament _____.
5. Number of books in the entire Bible _____.
6. Number of books in the Law division _____.
7. Number of main divisions of the entire Bible _____.

Consider God's Wonders

15

Choose two of these passages to read. Write on the lines provided the wonders of God that are listed in the passages you read.

Job 12:7-10
Psalm 19:1
Psalm 95:4-5

Psalm 104:5-23
Psalm 147:4-9
Psalm 148

Help Hanna

> Hi. Take a minute and help me. I took notes on the Bible story, but I'm not sure I've got everything right. Would you check them for me, please?

Elijah and the Still, Small Voice

1. Queen Jezebel threatened to have Elijah sent out of the country.

2. Elijah hired a camel caravan to take him to the desert.

3. After resting awhile, he went hunting for some food to eat.

4. He asked the camel caravan to take him on to Mt. Sinai.

5. At Mt. Sinai, Elijah told God that the Israelites had continued to worship Him, but they had no respect for the preachers.

6. God told Elijah to go stand on the mountain and quit feeling sorry for himself.

7. God spoke to Elijah through the wind, the earthquake, and the fire.

8. God told Elijah to go back and confront King Ahab and Queen Jezebel and maybe they would say they were sorry.

Bible Skills, Drills, & Thrills Activity Book Grades 4–6 Red Cycle
© 2014 LifeWay Press® Printed in the United States of America.

My Seed

Psalm 19:14 tells you to use your words to please God. Fill in the watermelon seed with words or phrases that you can say that would make God happy and proud of you. Work hard to use all of these words with your friends and family at school and at home this week.

Memory Signs

To the right are the sign language signs for some key words from your Bible verse. Learn two signs at a time. Recite your Bible verse each time you learn two key words. While you are reciting the verse, substitute the sign you have learned in place of those key words. Keep working hard until you know all of the key words in sign language and can say and sign the verse without looking at your activity page.

Words: Place the right index and thumb (with other fingers closed) against the left index which is pointing up, palm facing right.

Meditation: The index finger faces the forehead and makes a small circle.

Mouth: Point to the mouth.

Lord: Place the right "L" at the left shoulder, then on the right waist.

Redeem: Cross the "R" hands in front of you, palms facing in; then draw them to the sides in an "S" position, palm side out.

Add **Person Ending** to *Redeem* for *Redeemer*: Both open hands facing each other are brought down in front of the body.

Meeting 8

Psalm Puzzle

Milk Jug Catcher

Directions: Cut off the top and part of the front of a plastic milk jug to make a "milk jug catcher."

Use your Bible to find the answers to these questions:

1. How many chapters are there in the book of Psalms?

2. What is the longest Psalm?

3. How many chapters of Psalms have less than 10 verses?

4. Which Psalm begins with the words, "The Lord is my Shepherd"?

5. What is the shortest Psalm?

Forgiveness Bubbles

Psalm 51:1-5

Psalm 51:6-9

King David's Forgiveness

My Forgiveness

Psalm 51:18-19

Psalm 51:10-13

Psalm 51:14-17

Fix the Sentence

Meeting 9

Below you will find sentences that are incorrect. Read the Scripture reference, and fix the sentences.

Ready!   Set!   Go!

John 14:1-6

Thomas told Jesus, "No problem, we know where You're going!"

John 14:7-11

Philip told Jesus, "You cannot show us only your Father."

John 14:27-31

Jesus said, "You will have to be afraid after I leave you."

John 14:12-14

Jesus said, "If you ask in your name, God will be glorified."

John 14:19-25

Jesus said, "What I have said to you are My words alone."

Quilt Block of Comfort

Instructions

1. Place the dark three-inch square in the center of your nine-inch square paper.
2. Cut your medium value three-inch squares diagonally, from corner to corner.
3. Place the darkest of these triangles around your center square. Place them exactly like the pattern so that you will create a star.
4. Place the lightest of these triangles next to the triangle you just positioned to form a three-inch square.
5. Place your light three-inch squares in the four corners.
6. Carefully glue your pieces in place.
7. Write your new Key Passage—The Comfort Chapter: John 14, and your memory verse—Psalm 145:9 onto the light squares. Decorate the remaining squares with words such as peace or comfort.

Bible Skills, Drills, & Thrills Activity Book Grades 4–6 Red Cycle © 2014 LifeWay Press®--Printed in the United States of America.

Scrambled Eggs

Unscramble the words in the eggs below to discover things or people that will help you act wisely.

mlyFia

hacreesT

eraPyr

nretsaP

lbiBe

Toaster

BUTTER

Jelly

Each slice of toast contains a word from your memory verse or words that define a word from your memory verse. Decide which two pieces of toast belong together and then spread jelly on your toast by coloring your matching toast slices the same color.

discipline
training
teaching

Can apply knowledge to real life.

instruction

wise

Bible Skills, Drills, & Thrills Activity Book Grades 4–6 Red Cycle © 2014 LifeWay Press®._Printed in the United States of America.

Who's Watching You

Meeting 11

Everywhere you go, people are watching you. They see what you do and how you behave. Fill in the blanks below with names of people who watch you.

Stand Up

Proverbs 20:11 says that even children are known by their actions. What are some ways you can stand up for God?

Slip Into the Minor Prophets

Each of the slippers below contains the name of a book of Minor Prophets. Write the names of the books before and after each book on the lines provided. Take your activity page home and ask your parents to help you practice your Bible skills. Ask your parent to call out the middle book and let you find the book in your Bible and give the book before and the book after.

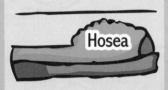
Hosea

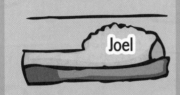
Joel

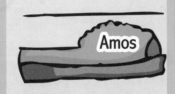
Amos

Nahum

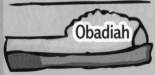
Obadiah

Jonah

Micah

Habakkuk

Zephaniah

Haggai

Zechariah

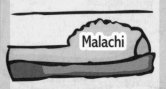
Malachi

Shipmate Signatures

■ Meeting 12   Try to fill your "Shipmate Signatures" grid with autographs. The signatures must not belong to a member of your family.

I love pizza.	Blue is my favorite color.	I like to sleep late.
I am a great swimmer.	I have memorized all of the memory verses for Bible Skills, Drills, & Thrills.	I read my Bible every day.
My mom is cool.	I am a rad skateboarder.	Mac and cheese is my favorite food.

Family Service

You have been learning how to serve others in Bible Skills, Drills, & Thrills. How can your family practice serving one another. Choose six Service projects that your family can work on at home. Fill in the service covenant below. Ask everyone to sign his/her name and serve one another with a smile.

Service Covenant

1. _____   4. _____

2. _____   5. _____

3. _____   6. _____

Family members sign here: _____   _____

_____   _____   _____

Bible Skills, Drills, & Thrills Activity Book Grades 4–6 Red Cycle © 2014 LifeWay Press®–Printed in the United States of America.

Meeting 13

Now You See It! Now You Don't!

Stare at the image of the red church while someone else keeps time with a second hand for 30 seconds. When the person calls time, quickly look up at a white wall or a white piece of paper. What do you see?

How many ways can you name to obey or worship God before the image you see on the paper fades?

Spheres of Influence

Me

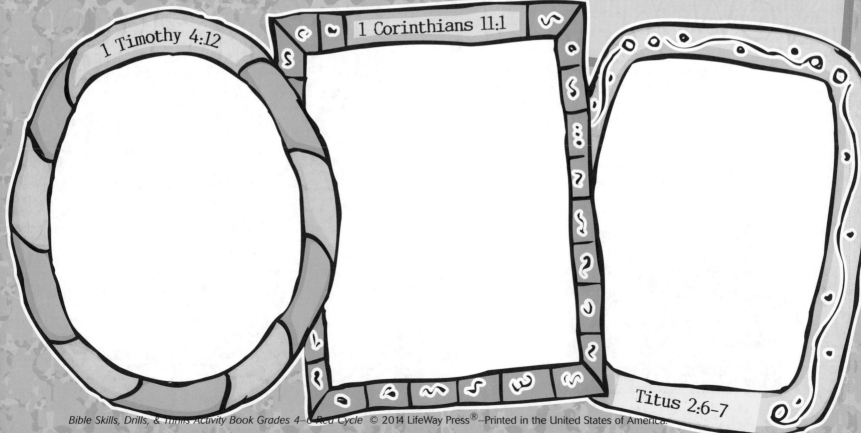

Model Behavior

Locate each of the verses in your Bible. Read the verse and put it in your own words. Write your answers on the mirrors. What kind of behavior does the Bible say you are to model?

1 Timothy 4:12

1 Corinthians 11:1

Titus 2:6-7

X-treme Code

Use the X-treme decoder to solve the coded message. The shape tells which point of the "X" to choose. The number tells how many letters to count along the leg of the "X" to find the correct letter.

————————————————————————— ,

☆3 ●5 ☆6 ●6   ☆7 ◻2 △4 ◻6

—————— —————— —————— —————— ——————
●6 △5 ●2 ◻3   ●5

—————— —————— —————— —————————————————
△3 △1 ◻1   ●2 ◻2 ☆4 △5

————————————————————————————————————— •
●1 ☆1   △5 ◻1 △5 ●1 ●5 △5 ◻6

To fulfill this assignment I need to

——————— ——————— •
◻3 ◻5 △1 ☆1

△ A B C D E F G
☆ (top right leg) T U V W X Y ★
S R Q P O N ◻ (bottom left)
G H I J K L M O (bottom right)

00=Z

"Thumper" Slide Gameboard

Challenge Grid . . . . .

Who
1. By yourself
2. All together
3. Everyone but you

What
1. Name the divisions of the Old Testament
2. Name the books of Law
3. Name the books of Old Testament History

How
1. In a squeaky voice.
2. In a booming voice.
3. In a whisper

Place a button or penny anywhere in the "Home" area. Thump the button to make it slide into the play area. Match the number code to the challenge grid. For example, if you land on "3-1-2," everyone but you would name the divisions of the Old Testament in a booming voice.

1-2-3   2-3-1   3-1-2   1-3-1   2-1-3   3-2-2   HOME

Bible Skills, Drills, & Thrills Activity Book Grades 4–6 Red Cycle © 2014 LifeWay Press®--Printed in the United States of America.

Meeting 15

Prayer Possibilities to Ponder

When do you like to pray?

Where do you like to pray?

How do you like to pray?

What do you often pray about?

Roly Poly Racer Gameboard

Name all the books of the Old Testament.

Quote a memory verse.

Name the five Old Testament divisions.

Top The Racer Bottom

Name two Key Passages (titles and references).

Locate a Gospel book in your Bible and name the books before and after.

Locate a Minor Prophet book in your Bible and name the books before and after.

Bible Skills, Drills, & Thrills Activity Book Grades 4–6 Red Cycle © 2014 LifeWay Press®--Printed in the United States of America.

Truths or Myths

Many books and movies tell the story about Jesus' birth, but which facts come from the Bible, which may have happened, and which are facts that aren't really facts at all?

The stories of Jesus' birth can be found in these passages:
Matthew 1:18-25, 2:1-12, Luke 2:1-20

Fact?	From the Bible	Possible, but the Bible doesn't say	Not a true fact.
Mary and Joseph were engaged.			
Mary rode on a donkey.			
The innkeeper offered the use of his stable.			
Mary wrapped the baby tightly in strips of cloth.			
The animals sang at midnight.			
There was a little drummer boy who came.			
Mary placed Baby Jesus in a manger.			
Three wise men came.			
The wise men's names were Gaspar, Balthasar, and Melchior.			

Family Focus Time

1. Read Matthew 1:20-21 and Luke 1:26-31.
How did Joseph and Mary learn that Jesus was going to be born?
How did your parents first learn that you were going to become a part of your family?

Prayer thought: Thank God for sending Jesus to live on earth as a human being in a human family.

2. Read Matthew 2:5-6 and Luke 2:1-5.
How did God use Caesar's decree to get Mary and Joseph to Bethlehem to fulfill God's prophecy?
Where was each member of your family born?

Prayer thought: Thank God that He kept His promise to send His Son, Jesus

3. Read Luke 2:7.
How did Mary care for the newborn Jesus? Ask your parents to tell about the day you were born or the day they brought you home.

Prayer thought: Thank God for all the ways He shows His love and care for you.

4. Read Isaiah 9:6.
How did Isaiah describe Jesus when he prophesied about Jesus' birth?
What words would you use to describe Jesus?

Prayer thought: Spend time praising Jesus for who He is and why He came to earth.

5. Read Luke 2:10-14.
What is your favorite part of the angel's message?
What do you think the shepherds might have been thinking?

Prayer thought: Thank God for sharing the good news about Jesus with your family.

6. Read Luke 2:21.
Why was He named *Jesus*?
How did your parents choose your name?

Prayer thought: The name *Jesus* means "Messiah" or "God Saves." Thank God for His plan to provide salvation.

7. Read John 3:16.
Why did God send Jesus to be born into a human family?
Why is this important to your family?

Prayer thought: Ask God to help your family tell others about Jesus.

In Someone Else's Shoes

Sam doesn't fit in with your friends, but he really wants to come to your birthday party.

Marcus always seems to have a bad day. He wants to call you after school, but all he does is complain!

Kelly can be so clumsy! She should have seen that you put your CD case on the floor before she stepped on it!

Morgan made fun of the way your hair looked yesterday. Today she fell and ripped a hole in her new jeans.

Something to Celebrate

Knowing how to become a Christian is something to celebrate. Each time another person accepts Jesus as his personal Savior, even the angels celebrate (Luke 15:10)!

From each banner find in your Bible one verse to read to a friend and ask the friend to initial your paper on that banner. Find another verse that you like from each banner, and print one of the three verses on each of the balloons.

A—Admit to God that you are a sinner. Repent, turning away from your sin.
Romans 3:23; Romans 6:23; Acts 3:19; 1 John 1:9

B—Believe that Jesus is God's Son and accept God's gift of forgiveness from sin.
Romans 5:8; Acts 4:12; John 3:16; John 14:6; Ephesians 2:8-9; John 1:11-13

C—Confess your faith in Jesus Christ as Savior and Lord.
Romans 10:9-10; Romans 10:13

Paul's Letters

How many names of Paul's letters can you remember? Fill in the blanks to complete the names. Don't forget! You will need to add a "1" or a "2" in front of six of the book names!

Bible Skills, Drills, & Thrills Activity Book Grades 4–6 Red Cycle © 2014 LifeWay Press®—Printed in the United States of America.

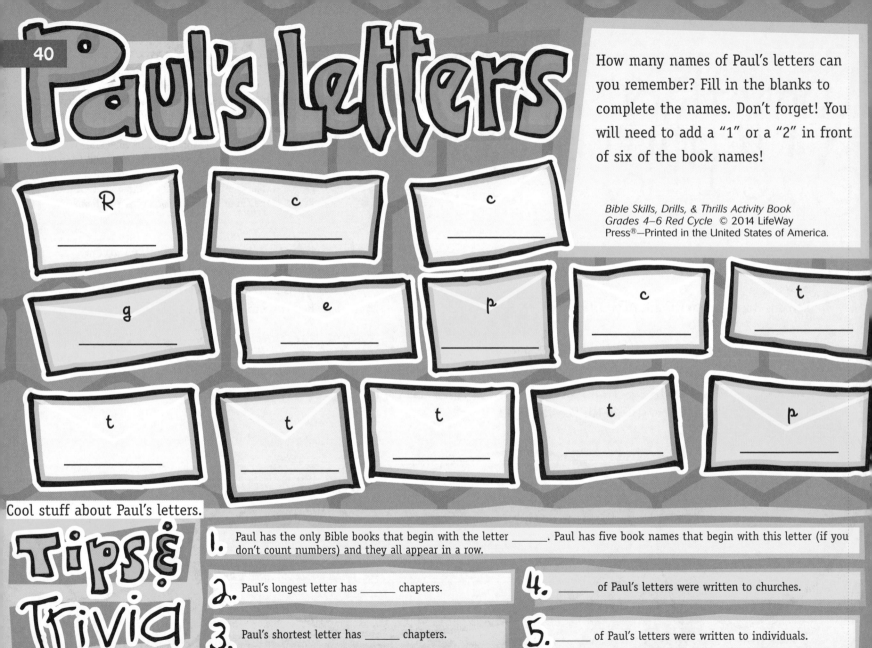

R _____

c _____

c _____

g _____

e _____

p _____

c _____

t _____

t _____

t _____

t _____

t _____

p _____

Cool stuff about Paul's letters.

Tips & Trivia

1. Paul has the only Bible books that begin with the letter _____. Paul has five book names that begin with this letter (if you don't count numbers) and they all appear in a row.

2. Paul's longest letter has _____ chapters.

3. Paul's shortest letter has _____ chapters.

4. _____ of Paul's letters were written to churches.

5. _____ of Paul's letters were written to individuals.

Bible Skills, Drills, & Thrills Activity Book Grades 4–6 Red Cycle © 2014 LifeWay Press®--Printed in the United States of America.

Plan of Salvation Reference: Psalm 139:13-16; Romans 5:8; John 3:16; John 14:6; Romans 3:23; Romans 10:9,13; 2 Corinthians 5:17

Men on Mission Interview Notes

Match the Key Passage to the correct reference. Check your answers in your Bible.

◼ Meeting 20

List all of the facts you learn about Paul and Silas.

Paul	Silas

Matching Mission

Key Passage	Reference
The Creation	Mark 12:28-34
The Greatest Commandments	Luke 15:11-32
The Israelites Leave Egypt	Genesis 1–2:3
A Prayer for Forgiveness	Luke 2:1-7
The Comfort Chapter	John 14
The Model Prayer	Exodus 12:37-42
The Birth of Jesus	Matthew 6:5-15
The Baptism of Jesus	Matthew 3:13-17
The Parable of the Prodigal Son	Psalm 51

Made for a Mission

Inside the outline of the child, list your talents and abilities. On the lines of the notebook paper, list ways you can develop your talents.

Print the names of different books of the Bible in each of the remaining squares. Spin the division spinner from "Game Spinners" (Pack Item 13). Cover all the Books of the Bible in that division on your grid. Continue playing until all the squares have been covered.

	Leviticus	
Hebrews		Proverbs
Ruth		Titus

Personal Testimonies

Testimony Tips

Talk to God about what to say in your testimony. Remember He Knows the story better than you do!

Tell the story with words people will understand.

Try telling your story to a friend first.

Bible Skills, Drills, & Thrills Activity Book Grades 4–6 Red Cycle © 2014 LifeWay Press®--Printed in the United States of America.

Frequent Flight Points

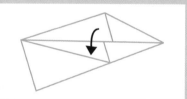

Meeting 22 · 47

Follow the instructions below to make a paper airplane. Fly your plane onto one of the runway strips marked with the divisions of the Bible. Name all of the books of the Bible in that division and receive 100 points for every correct answer. If you name all of the books correctly in that division, you receive a bonus of 1,000 points.

1

Fold the paper and crease it lengthwise.

2

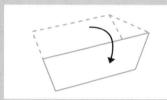

Fold one corner to the center.

3

Fold the other corner to the center.

4

Fold the paper in half.

5

Fold down one wing.

6

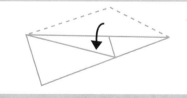

Fold down the other wing.

7

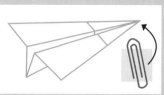

Fold the wings out. Add the paper clips to the nose.

8

Bend the back of the wing upward.

The Full Armor

Read the Key Passage:

The Christian's Armor in Ephesians 6:10-20.
Label each of the parts of the armor with
the Bible verse as you study the Bible
during Group Skills.

Bible Skills, Drills, & Thrills Activity Book
Grades 4–6 Red Cycle © 2014 LifeWay Press®--
Printed in the United States of America.

Book Work

Read Acts 18:3, 18–28.
Fill in the correct answers using the words from the scrambled word box.

1. Paul, Priscilla, and Aquila were _____.
2. Priscilla and Aquila left with Paul to go to _____.
3. _____ left Priscilla and Aquila and continued on his trip.
4. _____ was an eloquent man and was knowledgeable of the Scriptures.
5. _____ and _____ heard him speak in the synagogue.
6. The married couple took him aside to _____.
7. Apollos quickly began teaching others about _____.

usseJ

slopAlo

theac

luaP

ayrSi

sreknmttea

sciiPrlla

qiaulA

Circle the **T** if the statement is true. Circle the **F** if the statement is false.

T or **F** The Bible story is found in the Book of Acts.

T or **F** The Book of Acts is located in the Old Testament History division of the Bible.

T or **F** Priscilla an Aquila heard Apollos speak in the synagogue.

T or **F** Priscilla and Aquila corrected Apollos in the synagogue.

T or **F** Priscilla and Aquila encouraged Apollos.

T or **F** Apollos wanted to teach others what he had learned about Jesus.

Write Your Name on the Board

Write your name on the board.
Next to each letter, write character traits that begin with that letter.

Technical Difficulties

Bible Drill Techniques

The mistakes in the video are:

-1. The child fails to step out within 10 seconds.
2. The child gives the incorrect response. This includes any child who raises his or her hand, indicating an error.
3. The child fails to stand straight or keep his eyes on the drill caller until the command "Start" is given.
4. When the Bible is used, the child steps forward before the index finger is on the correct response.
5. The child fails to handle the Bible according to instructions or obviously misuses the Bible. The Bible should be parallel to the floor with one hand flat on the top and one hand flat on the bottom with no fingers extending over the edges.

1 Stand straight and keep your eyes on the drill caller until the command "start" is given.

2 Place your index finger on the correct response before stepping forward.

3 "Attention" means to stand straight with your hands at your side.

4 Hold the Bible flat with no fingers extending over the edges.

5 Once you step out, don't go back. If you have made a mistake, raise your hand.

6 Speak loudly and slowly so the judges can hear and understand you.

7 If you have started out when time is called, come on out. Let the judge decide if you were in time.

8 Do not step out if you don't know the answer.

9 Treat your Bible with respect.

Family Flight Plans

Choose a family service project from this list or think of one of your own.

Neighborhood Needs

Look for an opportunity to serve one of your neighbors. Consider doing yard work for an elderly neighbor, babysitting for a busy neighbor, a dinner for a sick neighbor, or a welcome bag for a new neighbor.

Church Chores

Talk with a leader at your church to plan a day at the church to complete chores such as cleaning preschool toys, organizing the supply closets in the children's departments, stocking the kitchen pantry, or completing administrative tasks for upcoming events.

Preschool Plan

Talk with the preschool director of a local school. Get a list of supplies or services that could be donated to them to help enhance the learning environment for the preschool children.

Community Clutter

Plan a cleanup mission for a local park or other area of your neighborhood.

Animal Assistance

Call a local animal shelter. Get a list of supplies or services that could be donated to them to help them care for the animals.

Bible Skills, Drills, & Thrills Activity Book Grades 4–6 Red Cycle © 2014 LifeWay Press®--Printed in the United States of America.

Family Time

Meeting 25

You can honor your parents in no time! Or you can honor them for a long time. Either way, think of some ways you can honor and obey your parents that take up these times:

Honor: To show respect for a person or to cherish a person.

obey: To carry out someone's instructions.

30 seconds _____

15 minutes _____

1 minute _____

30 minutes _____

5 minutes _____

1 hour _____

Who's Job is it anyway?

Parent's Job	Children's Job
Genesis 18:19	Leviticus 19:3
Proverbs 13:24	Proverbs 1:8
Proverbs 22:6	Proverbs 4:20
Ephesians 6:4	Ephesians 6:1
1 Timothy 3:4	Philippians 2:14

Family Contract

Family Contract

Because we believe that God says families should _____

,the _____ Family enters into this contract.

As parents, we will do our best to _____
_____
_____

As the child, I will do my best to _____
_____
_____

_____

We agree to this contract on _____.
　　　　　　　　　　　　　　　　　　(date)

Parent's signature_____

Child's signature_____

An Exciting Chain of Events

Who says being a missionary is dull? Check out Paul's adventures, as he described them, in 2 Corinthians 11:24-27.

Circle the adventures that Paul mentioned in those verses. Cross out any links that don't belong.

Experts think Paul traveled about **17,300 miles** in his lifetime: that's equal to more than halfway around the world!

Paul was given 39 lashes by the Jews.

Paul hid in a bear's den for 30 days.

Paul was beaten with rods.

Paul spent a day and night on the open sea.

Paul was shipwrecked three times.

Paul was stoned.

Paul was forced to be a gladiator.

Paul was in the Great Fire of Rome.

Paul was endangered by robbers.

Paul often went without food and clothing.

What makes you strong during tough times?

What was Paul's secret for being content?

Where was Paul when he wrote to the Philippian church?

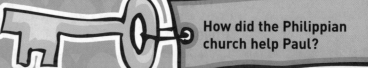

How did the Philippian church help Paul?

Map Matics
Paul's Letters Traveled to From

Follow the tangled paths to discover where Paul was
when he wrote his letters, and where his letters traveled.
(Some locations may appear more than once.)

Paul's Letters

Romans
1 Corinthians
2 Corinthians
Galatians
Ephesians
Philippians
Colossians
1 Thessalonians
2 Thessalonians
1 Timothy
2 Timothy
Titus
Philemon

Traveled to

Galatia
Philippi
Colossae
Thessalonica
Crete
Corinth
Ephesus
Rome

From

Antioch
Ephesus
Rome
Macedonia
Corinth
Rome or Macedonia

Ice Breaker

Can you break (color in) five ice blocks in a row, across, up and down, or diagonally before your opponent does? Here's how to play:

1. Choose any square in the iceberg.
2. Follow the row across and down.
3. If you can name an Old Testament book and a New Testament book that begins with the letters you found in each row and column the block is yours. Color it in.

Take turns, and don't forget to block your opponent's blocks!

Old Testament

E
Z
L
S
P
N
I
R
J
G

New Testament

H T P E G C M A L R

Monstrous Meltdowns

Hot tempers nearly always cause a monster meltdown! Give an example of these wrong ways to handle anger:

Bible Skills, Drills, & Thrills Activity Book Grades 4–6 Red Cycle © 2014 LifeWay Press®–Printed in the United States of America.

How to Get MAD!

Revenge
Hurting someone who has hurt or embarrassed you.

Malice
Harming or hurting someone without just cause.

Agitation
To be upset or annoyed by something small or unimportant.

Bitterness
Holding a grudge for a long time.

Resentment
Anger toward someone that affects your actions toward that person.

Dissension
Disagreement or disloyalty to a person or people.

Slander
Hateful talk about someone you dislike.

Give Em A Hand!

From Here to There

Draw an arm that reaches from the Bible book to the description of its writer.

Mark

Luke

Romans

James

Revelation

Written by a doctor who traveled with Paul on some of Paul's missionary journeys.

Written by a former fisherman who was sometimes called "the disciple Jesus loved."

Written by a man who once tried to destroy the followers of Jesus.

Written by the earthly half brother of Jesus.

Written by a young man who caused a disagreement between Paul and Barnabas after he left them in the middle of a missionary trip.

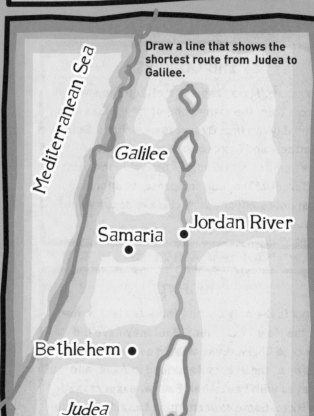

Draw a line that shows the shortest route from Judea to Galilee.

Mediterranean Sea

Galilee

Jordan River

Samaria

Bethlehem

Judea

X-tra Information

This x-ray added too many X's! See if you can understand the x-tra information about the New Testament!

The Gospels

Mxxxxxw, Mxxx, and Lxxx, all tell the story of Jxxxs from the same point of view. Mxxx was probably the first Gxxxxl to be written. Both Matthew and Lxxx contain stories that are not found in Mxxx. John's Gxxxxl is the most different of the four and presents information that only someone very close to Jesus would be able to share.

Paul's Letter

Most of Paul's lettxxs are written to chxrxxes that he had helped start. Some of Paul's lexxxrs are full of encourxxxment. Others contain warnings to church members who were disobxxxent. Some letters were to specific Christian friends like Tixxxhy, xxtus, and Philxxxx.

Prophecy

John wrote Rxxxlation from the islxxd of Patmos, where he had been exiled. John used vivid word pictures and stories to describe Jexxs' rxxurn and the final defxxt of Satan.

History

Lxxx is the only Gentile (non-Jewish) writer in the New Txxxxment. Paul may have led Lxxx to Christ. Luke was an eyewixxxss to many of the events described in Axxs, and stayed with Paul when Paul was ixprxsxxed in Rxxe. Some experts think Lxxx planned to write a third book besides the Gxxxxl of Lxxx and Axxs.

General Letters

The writer of Hexxxxs is unknown. xames was a half-brother to Jesus. Pxxxr encouraged his Christian friends to have courxxe when they were persecuted. John wrote that Christians should show Jesus' lxxe to others. Juxx was also a half-brother of Jesus.

Bible Skills, Drills, & Thrills Activity Book Grades 4–6 Red Cycle © 2014 LifeWay Press®–Printed in the United States of America.

"Shake and Quake"

Bunny Buddies

Richter Scale | My Scale

Earthquakes are measured on the Richter scale, as you can see below. How do you measure your fears? Fill in the scale from:
1 (kiddy stuff) to
10 (shake-in-your-boots scary).

10: Huge cracks in the ground, landslides.

9: Sturdy buildings collapse.

8: Weak buildings collapse.

7: Hard to stand.

6: Plaster cracks.

5: Buildings and trees shake.

4: Can be felt indoors.

3: Vibrates like a passing car.

2: Can be felt on upper floors.

1: Barely noticeable.

My Scale

10 _____

9 _____

8 _____

7 _____

6 _____

5 _____

4 _____

3 _____

2 _____

1 _____

Here's how to make a bunny buddy to share with a terrified toddler:

1. Lay a washcloth on the table with the point toward yourself.

2. Roll two corners evenly toward the center.

3. Bend the washcloth in half. The loose ends will be the bunny's ears.

4. Bend the folded part of the washcloth toward you. Wrap a rubber band around the bundle you just made.

5. Flip the bundle over. Tug gently on the bunny's ears to separate them.

6. Glue on wiggly eyes and a pom-pom nose and tail.

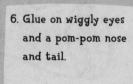

Storm Stories

The Gospels contain several storm stories—and Jesus was in control in all of them! Pick one of these and draw a story strip that tells the tale.

Matthew 8:23-27   Matthew 14:22-33

Mark 4:35-41   Luke 8:22-25

Meeting 30

Read Between the Lines

Sixteen Bible books are hidden in this news story. Some inside words; some are between words. How many can you find?

Community Cooking Up Cooking Contest

Numbers of people will compete really heavily in a most interesting contest this weekend. Yes, there will be crowds of people watching the second annual "Frog Leg Fricassee" held at the local market.

Judges will award prizes to the creative cook who fries up the best frog leg recipe.

Lulu Kerfriddle, last year's winner, shared the truth behind her secret frog leg formula: "Everybody makes a supper recipe. My husband and I fry up a frog leg breakfast! It's a two-person job. He brews the coffee while I fry up the legs like bacon. That's a fact. Some people try to fry up the frog legs alone, but you can get yourself in a jam, especially if you're trying to cook up an omelet at the same time. I admit it usually doesn't take both of us to cook at home, but we want to make sure that plate of fresh frog legs is looking so good."

The public is invited for the revelation of this year's Frog Leg Fricassee champion, and the lamentations of the losing cooks.

Across
3. You can collect f___. (James 2:15–16)
4. You can be a w___ for Jesus. (Acts 1:8)
6. You can share c___. (Luke 3:11)
8. You can p___ for all kinds of people (1 Timothy 2:1)

Down
1. You can show h___. (Romans 12:13)
2. When you s___ others, you s___ the Lord. (Romans 12:11)
5. You can be kind to a little c___. (Mark 10:14)
7. You can visit a s___ person. (Matthew 25:36)

63

Help Wanted

Lost Axe Head!

Need replacement for borrowed iron axe head that dropped into the Jordan River.
Please see 2 Kings 6:1-7.

Thirsty Camels Need a Drink.

Hard working animal lover needed to draw gallons and gallons of water for ten camels who carried gifts and supplies across the desert. Look for owner at Genesis 24:1-21.

Seeking a Seamstress.

Poor widows and orphans in desperate need of clean, good-fitting clothing. Need kind seamstress, willing to donate material and supplies. Please apply at Acts 9:36-43.

Wise Woman Needed.

Wife with good judgment and common sense needed to provide food for David and approximately 600 men when foolish husband turns the fighters away.
Contact the following for details:
1 Samuel 25:3-19

Excellent Penmanship? Apply Here!

Dedicated scribe needed to record a prophet's messages from the Lord. No computer available; all work must be done by hand. Must be willing to put life at risk in order to read the message to the king's helpers. Overtime may be necessary in case of fire.
See Jeremiah 36:1-6,16-19, 27-32

Table Servers Needed

Diplomatic, hard-working, godly men needed to serve food to Greek Jews. Must have a good reputation and be full of the Spirit.
See Acts 6:1-7.

Meeting 31
A Word of Advice

Fill in the crossword puzzle spaces with the correct answers. Use your Bible if you need help.

Across:
1. The book before Proverbs.
3. Two books after the two Samuels.
5. The third Gospel.
7. The two books just before Titus.

Down:
2. The second Gospel.
4. The book after Micah.
6. The book after Galatians

Write the letters that are in circles here. Unscramble the letters to discover a two word hidden message.
(Hint: The second word is only two letters long.)

Find Proverbs 8:33 in your Bible and see if the advice given is good advice.

Getting Good Advice

List people you can rely on to give you good advice. Circle the ones you have asked for advice in the past.

Read each situation. Think about the problem. In the space provided list who could give you good advice and what advice you think they might give.

You are lost at the mall.

You don't understand a verse in the Bible.

Your best friend moved away and you are lonely.

You are having trouble with math class.

Who Do I Respect?

Meeting 32

Listed in each box are some of the people you should respect. The names are scrambled. Unscramble each name and in the space provided, write at least one way you can show respect to that person.

RSAPOT	DRELES	CHERAET	CAHE HEROT	VEMONGTENR LAFFOICI

LOPEMANIC	DRAFILEGU	IFLYAM BREMMES	STRAPEN	SLYFEM

Write one way you will show respect this week.

Lessons Learned from David

David showed respect to King Saul. David spent a lot of time hiding in caves and running from King Saul until he finally became the king of Israel. He learned many lessons and wrote them in the book of Psalms. Find each of the following verses in your Bible. Write in your own words what you can learn from David's words. Encourage your family members to find the verses with you.

Psalm 16:11		Psalm 27:1	

Psalm 18:1-3		Psalm 40:1-3	

Psalm 25:4-6		Psalm 54:4,7	

Bible Skills, Drills, & Thrills Activity Book Grades 4–6 Red Cycle © 2014 LifeWay Press®–Printed in the United States of America.

Scene 1: Deborah Rallies the Troops

The Cast

Narrator

Children of Israel

Israelite

Voice of the Lord

Deborah

Barak

Deborah Rallies the Troops

Narrator: Once again the Israelites did evil in the sight of the Lord and so they were sold into the hand of Jabin, king of Canaan. Jabin ruled the Israelites harshly for 20 years with the help of Sisera, his army commander. The children of Israel finally cried out to God for help.

Children of Israel: (All on their knees as if praying) Dear God, please help us. Help us defeat Jabin and Sisera.

Israelite: Help us, Lord, for Jabin has 900 iron chariots. We need your help.

Narrator: And so the Lord heard their cries and called on Barak to gather the troops of Israel for battle.

Voice of the Lord: Barak, I want you to gather 10,000 men and prepare for battle for I will bring Sisera to you. I will hand him over to you.

Barak: I heard you Lord, but I can't go.

Narrator: Barak did not immediately do what God had commanded him to do, so the Lord spoke to Deborah who was the judge of Israel at that time. Deborah would sit under the palm trees and judge the people. The Lord told Deborah to talk to Barak.

Deborah: Go and bring Barak to me that I may talk to him.

(Barak will enter and bow before Deborah and then stand up.)

Deborah: Barak, hasn't God told you to gather 10,000 troops and go and fight against Jabin and Sisera? Did God not tell you that He would hand Sisera over to you?

Barak: Yes, Deborah. If you will go with me, I will go. But if you will not go with me, I will not go.

Deborah: I will help you, Barak, to rally our troops and go into battle. God will help us defeat our enemy.

Narrator: And so Deborah agreed to go into battle against Sisera and his men. Barak did gather the 10,000 troops like the Lord commanded and went against the army of Jabin. The Israelites were victorious and defeated Jabin and Sisera with God's help.

An Account of Me

Knowing God's Will

The best place to find the will of God is in His Word. Read the following verses in your Bible, and in the spaces provided briefly state what the will of God is according to the verse.

Matthew 22:37	John 13:34	Ephesians 4:32	Ephesians 6:1	Philippians 4:4	1 Thessalonians 5:17	1 Thessalonians 5:18

Bible Skills, Drills, & Thrills Activity Book Grades 4–6 Red Cycle © 2014 LifeWay Press®–Printed in the United States of America

My Daily Account

List five things that you now know are the will of God. *(Use the verses from above to help you. Check with your leader if you are unsure.)* Make a mark for each time you follow God's will in your life this week. At the end of the week add up the total number of times you followed God's will.

God's Will	Sun	Mon	Tues	Wed	Thurs	Fri	Sat	Total

HOW DO YOU FEEL?

Find Luke 6:37 in your Bible and write the words and reference on the lines below.

Look at each picture below. Think about a situation in your life that goes with each picture—a time someone judged you, a time you were condemned *(punished)*, and a time you were forgiven. Draw a picture in the circle under each picture that shows how you felt during that time.

I find you guilty.

I am here for 30 days.

Father, forgive them.

Judge

Condemn

Forgive

I felt...

I felt...

I felt...

Case Study

Bible Skills, Drills, & Thrills Activity Book Grades 4–6 Red Cycle
© 2014 LifeWay Press®–Printed in the United States of America.

It's your birthday and everyone has gathered at your house for a big party. You are wearing your new clothes and want everything to be just right. One of your friends starts telling everyone that he can play the video game better than you. He keeps on teasing you even though you tell him that this is the first time you have ever played the game. When you finally catch on and start beating him, he tries to grab the control away from you, knocking fruit punch all over your new clothes. Everyone starts laughing, but you are mad and hurt toward your friend. What should you do?

Steps to Forgiveness

Unscramble the key words in each step. Read what you might say to your friend.

		Answers·
Step 1	Make the first <u>ovem</u>. "Let's talk about what just happened."	
Step 2	State how you <u>efle</u>. "What you did hurt my feelings and made me angry, but I am willing to forgive you and give you another chance."	
Step 3	Accept your <u>renifd</u>. "I still want us to be friends."	
Step 4	<u>grofte</u> about the incident. "I will not bring it up again."	

Find these verses about forgiveness in your Bible and write them in the boxes provided

EPHESIANS 4:32	MATTHEW 6:12	COLOSSIANS 3:12-13

Meeting 35
Find the Books

Highlighter Colors for Divisions:

Gospels–Green   **History**–Yellow

Paul's Letters–Orange   **General Letters**–Pink

Prophecy–Blue

Search for the books of the New Testament. The books may be found horizontally, vertically, or diagonally. When you have located a book, use a highlighter to mark the book according to the division where it is found. Use the color code to the right.

```
X O M A T T H E W A C R 2 G V C E 2
B 1 J O H N R T G B O W J A 2 E S C
A S D F M G H J K L L I O L P H J O
S N A I T A L A G R O N H A E K 1 R
E R F T 1 P E T E R S O N T T I T I
M A T M T W O E D V S I Z I E K H N
A X R T I G B S U D I T E A R X E T
N C T I T O P N J M A A H A C Q S H
C V T B U G E A W S N L M A F G S I
H T R S S D E M D E S E J L I N A A
Y W E D C B N I L R E V I L H H L N
H E B R E W S R E V R E N O S T O S
T E P H E S I A N S W R J E A E N C
O 2 T I M O T H Y Y L 3 E K U L I R
M Q U B S E C N O M E L I H P L A E
I Z C B E T 1 C O R I N T H I A N S
T W A N M A D O L I M Y B I B L S V
1 W H C A U R O M A N S H R S W R C
O O C V J P H I L I P P I A N S D K
J O H N 2 T H E S S A L O N I A N S
```

Will You Stand Alone?

Read each case study.
Review the discussions questions
and be prepared to answer with
your group.

Case Study 1—There's A New Kid in Town

Jordan and his friends were sitting at their usual table in the lunchroom when the principal entered the room with a new kid. Jordan noticed that the new kid did not appear very happy, and even looked as if he might cry. Joshua's friends began to give each other sly looks and to snicker. One boy said, "I hope he doesn't come over here." Before he had finished speaking, Mr. Jones and the new kid were coming toward their table. As he approached, Mr. Jones said: "Boys, I'd like you to meet Ashton. This is Ashton's first day, and I thought he could sit here with you guys." The principal turned to leave and as Ashton started to sit down, one of the other boys pulled the chair out from under him and Ashton hit the floor. All of the students in the cafeteria saw what happened and began to laugh. Ashton stood up quickly and ran out of the room in tears. Jordan felt bad about what had happened and stood up.

Questions to Consider

-• What do you think Jordan did?
-• What would you have done?
-• How could you have stood up against the rest of the kids who were laughing?
-• Would it be hard or difficult to stand up against the rest of your friends who were laughing?

Case Study 2—A Trip to the Mall

It was Mary's birthday and for her party she and five friends were planning a sleepover. The girls met at the mall to watch a movie before going back to Mary's house. After the movie, they were to wait inside the drugstore until Mary's mom came to pick them up. The girls looked around the make-up aisle deciding on what different colors of nail polish to buy when Joanie suggested they didn't have to buy it all. "Why not take it? It's just a cheap bottle of nail polish. They'll never miss a few. Just slide it in your pocket." The girls looked at each other and then around the store. No one was anywhere near them so one by one they each chose a color and slipped it into their pockets. Joanie asked Mary what color she wanted. Mary knew that this was stealing, but all of the girls seemed to be going along with the idea.

Questions to Consider

-• What do you think Mary did?
-• What would you have done?
-• How could you take a stand in a case like this?
-• How hard would it be to stand against your friends who were going to be spending the night with you?

Meeting 36

My Trip Diary

Take a moment to fill in the trip diary highlighting some of your favorite parts of *Bible Skills, Drills, & Thrills*. Share with your parents what you write in your diary.

Start

1 Dear Diary,
My favorite verse this year is

2 Dear Diary,
My favorite game we played was

3 Dear Diary,
I really like our leader because

4 Dear Diary,
My friend _____ comes to the meetings with me. I like _____ because

5 Dear Diary,
My favorite Bible story is

6 Dear Diary,
It's been a great year in Bible Skills, Drills, & Thrills because

END

RoadTrip!

Follow each direction when you see the following road signs along the way on your trip or vacation. Check off each sign when you complete the activity.

Bible Skills, Drills, & Thrills Activity Book Grades 4–6 Red Cycle
© 2014 LifeWay Press®–Printed in the United States of America.

Name the books of History in the Old Testament.

Find Obadiah in your Bible.

Name the books of the Major Prophets.

Name the books of Paul's Letters.

Find 2 Corinthians in your Bible.

What is the reference for The Comfort Chapter?

What is the reference for The Model Prayer?

Quote Proverbs 8:33 or locate it in your Bible and read it aloud.

Name the books of the New Testament in order.

Books of the Old Testament

Law
Genesis Exodus Leviticus Numbers Deuteronomy

History
Joshua	1 Chronicles
Judges	2 Chronicles
Ruth	Ezra
1 Samuel	Nehemiah
2 Samuel	Esther
1 Kings	
2 Kings	

Poetry
Job
Psalms
Proverbs
Ecclesiastes
Song of
Solomon
(Songs)

Major Prophets
Isaiah
Jeremiah
Lamentations
Ezekiel
Daniel

Minor Prophets
Hosea	Nahum
Joel	Habakkuk
Amos	Zephaniah
Obadiah	Haggai
Jonah	Zechariah
Micah	Malachi

Books of the New Testament

Gospels
Matthew Mark Luke John

History
Acts

Paul's Letters
Romans	1 Thessalonians
1 Corinthians	2 Thessalonians
2 Corinthians	1 Timothy
Galatians	2 Timothy
Ephesians	Titus
Philippians	Philemon
Colossians	

General Letters
Hebrews	1 John
James	2 John
1 Peter	3 John
2 Peter	Jude

Prophecy
Revelation

Skill Check List

❑ Knows Books of the Bible
❑ Old Testament
  ❑ Books of Law
  ❑ Books of History
  ❑ Books of Poetry
  ❑ Books of Major Prophets
  ❑ Books of Minor Prophets
❑ New Testament
  ❑ Books of Gospels
  ❑ Book of History
  ❑ Books of Paul's Letters
  ❑ Books of General Letters
  ❑ Book of Prophecy

❑ Knows Bible Verses
❑ 1. Genesis 1:27
❑ 2. Leviticus 22:31
❑ 3. Deuteronomy 6:5
❑ 4. 1 Chronicles 16:8
❑ 5. Job 37:14
❑ 6. Psalm 19:14
❑ 7. Psalm 54:2
❑ 8. Psalm 145:9
❑ 9. Proverbs 8:33
❑ 10. Proverbs 20:11
❑ 11. Micah 6:8
❑ 12. Matthew 5:44
❑ 13. Matthew 21:22
❑ 14. Mark 13:31
❑ 15. Luke 6:31
❑ 16. John 8:32
❑ 17. John 15:13
❑ 18. Acts 1:8
❑ 19. Romans 14:12
❑ 20. 1 Corinthians 10:31
❑ 21. 1 Corinthians 14:40
❑ 22. Ephesians 6:1
❑ 23. Philippians 4:13
❑ 24. James 1:19
❑ 25. 1 John 4:19

❑ Knows Bonus Verses
❑ Psalm 46:1
❑ Matthew 25:40
❑ Luke 6:37

❑ Knows Key Passages
❑ The Creation:
  Genesis 1–2:3
❑ The Israelites Leave Egypt:
  Exodus 12:37-42
❑ A Prayer for Forgiveness:
  Psalm 51
❑ The Baptism of Jesus:
  Matthew 3:13-17
❑ The Model Prayer:
  Matthew 6:5-15
❑ The Great Commandments:
  Mark 12:28-34
❑ The Birth of Jesus:
  Luke 2:1-7
❑ The Parable of the Prodigal Son:
  Luke 15:11-32
❑ The Comfort Chapter:
  John 14
❑ The Christian's Armor:
  Ephesians 6:10-20

Name:_____